SEGREGATION

SEGREGATION: FEDERAL POLICY OR RACISM?
Copyright © 2017 by John Chodes

ALL RIGHTS RESERVED. No part of this publication may be reproduced, distributed, or transmitted in any form or by any means, including photocopying, recording, or other electronic or mechanical methods, or by any information storage and retrieval system without the prior written permission of the publisher, except in the case of very brief quotations embodied in critical reviews and certain other non-commercial uses permitted by copyright law.

Produced in the REPUBLIC OF SOUTH CAROLINA by

SHOTWELL PUBLISHING, LLC
Post Office Box 2592
Columbia, South Carolina 29202

www.ShotwellPublishing.com

Cover Design: Hazel's Dream

ISBN-13: 978-1947660007
ISBN-10: 1947660004

10 9 8 7 6 5 4 3 2 1

SEGREGATION

FEDERAL POLICY or RACISM?

JOHN CHODES

Shotwell Publishing
Columbia, South Carolina

Contents

Preface vii

Introduction ix

I. The Slave South: An Integrated Society 1

II. The Slave South: An Integrated Military 6

III. Presidential Reconstruction: The South Still Integrated 11

IV. Congressional Reconstruction: Segregation Begins 16

V. The Union League: Segregation Through Terror 26

VI. The Freedmen's Bureau: Segregation for Black Education 34

VII. The Morrill Act: Segregating Whites for Re-Education 43

VIII. The Bureau of Education: Nationalizing Segregation 53

IX. Segregation by Fusing Church and State 59

X. Conclusion: Reconstruction Continues Into the 21st Century 68

Preface

JOHN CHODES is a prolific author and an iconoclastic historian with a libertarian bent. He is dissatisfied with the increasing authoritarianism, invasion of individual rights, and culture wrecking that we have experienced with the American federal government in the last half century or more. Although a lifelong New Yorker and a resident of Manhattan, Chodes has found his way to the thought of the South as a base of criticism for current evils. This may be surprising to some, but perhaps not to those of us who are familiar with the prophetic power of the Southern critique of wrong roads taken by the American elite.

Chodes has previously published works, among others, on the grievous persecution of Northerners who refused to go along with Lincoln's war on the Southern people and the Constitution — one of the bigger untold stories of American history. Also, revisionist works on the tangled story of "Reconstruction." (See his *Washington's KKK* published by Shotwell and his book on J.L.M. Curry and New South education.)

"Segregation" and the federal government campaign to eradicate it has been a very large subject of recent times. But what if the government that now denounces separation of the races in the South is the same government that played a major role in establishing segregation amidst the ruins of the conquered land after its lost war for independence? If that is so, as Chodes persuasively shows, then we will, if honest, have to seriously revise the history of the subject.

"Reconstruction" is the most contentious period of American history. For a long time, it was taken for granted by mainstream historians that Reconstruction was a tragic mistake — that it was too harsh, vindictive, irrational, stupendously corrupt, and left a bitter legacy. More recently, a different view has become mainstream: Reconstruction was a noble effort of black Americans and their friends to establish true equality and democracy that was ultimately defeated by the reactionary violence of the Southern white ruling class. The Marxist cast of this interpretation is evident.

In *Segregation* Chodes has most pertinently explored neglected aspects of "Reconstruction" and restored a truer historical perspective. And this work is genuinely "relevant" to the present day because the author shows how many of our ills originate in that evil regime.

—*Shotwell Publishing*

Introduction

SEGREGATION. The very word resounds powerfully through contemporary America. It provokes images of all that is supposedly evil and unequal in the Southern mind: Bull Connor, with his megaphone and snarling dogs in Birmingham, Alabama; fire hoses knocking down freedom marchers; Jim Crow laws with signs reading "white only" and "colored only"; separate and unequal education; separate and unequal employment; blacks as second-class citizens.

Contemporary Americans assume, without hesitation, that segregation is the result of racism and white supremacy, and is still a lingering legacy of the antebellum slave society. The Civil War, Reconstruction, and 150-plus years of progressive education have not yet erased that evil legacy. Once a racist, always a racist, or so it seems.

Yet this story, so imprinted into the American psyche as we near the end of the second decade of the 21st century, is an inaccurate one. It is yet another example of how the Federal government, by controlling education through subsidies to book publishers over the past century, has erased the true history of our nation. Instead, a politically correct egalitarian history has been substituted. It is at odds with the truth.

James and Walter Kennedy, in *The South Was Right!*, said it most clearly when they quoted from the classic, *I'll Take My Stand*, published in 1930, in which Twelve Southerners defended the South and its agrarian tradition. Frank L. Owsley contributed a section titled "The Irrepressible Conflict":

> Northerners attempted to recast every opinion opposed to the North's myths, to impose Northern ways upon the Southern people, to ... write error across the pages of Southern history which were out of keeping with the Northern legend, and set the rising and unborn generations upon stools of everlasting repentance ... the rising generations were to receive the proper education in the Northern tradition. ... The rising generations read Northern literature, shot through with the New England tradition. Northern textbooks were used in Southern schools; Northern histories, despite the frantic protests of local patriotic organizations, were almost universally taught in Southern high schools and colleges – books that were built around the Northern legends and either completely ignored the South or insisted upon the unrighteousness of most of its history.[1]

This new history erased the fact that segregation is not the result of Southern racism. It is the result of federal policy from 1865 to 1900 to divide the white and black races and to promote discord and hatred for political advantage. This work demonstrates the process of federal segregation through the following sections:

I. *The Slave South: An Integrated Society*. Even during the slave era, Southern society was not segregated. It was integrated. Not by love, but by necessity. The black and white races needed each other in order to survive and prosper. They lived together, cheek-by-jowl. They were mutually dependent. All this changed with the defeat of the Confederacy and the rise of Radical

Republicanism during Congressional Reconstruction. Then this was transformed, by the bayonet, into mutual suspicion and loathing, separation, and violence. A great mental and physical chasm opened up between the races.

II. *The Slave South: An Integrated Military*. Contrary to politically correct history, the Confederacy used blacks, slave and free, as troops, long before the North did. Slaves were integrated with white troops into Southern armies. Northern black troops were segregated. Slaves formed a portion of Confederate armed forces.

III. *Presidential Reconstruction: South Still Integrated*. For the first two years after the end of the War for Southern Independence, under Presidential Reconstruction, Southern society remained integrated. Under Andrew Johnson's leadership, moderation, reconciliation and restoration were the policies pursued.

IV. *Congressional Reconstruction: Segregation Begins*. Congress overturned Johnson's policies and systematically divided the South into racially segregated societies. The old order was inverted by force so that whites were legally and politically inferior to blacks.

In many respects, the Reconstruction-era policy of divide and conquer is still maintained today but in a subtler form.

This process began in 1867 with the transition from restoration of the South to the Union to Radical Congressional Reconstruction. This period produced two destructive Constitutional amendments; the 14th and 15th.

The 14th Amendment gave civil rights to blacks and took away rights from "traitorous" whites. The 15th Amendment gave blacks voting powers. Both these amendments drove a tremendous antagonistic wedge between the races. They were not intended to create equality between the blacks and whites, they were to put the bottom rail on the top and perpetuate constant discord, violence, and political submission of the rebels to the freedmen. These Constitutional amendments were acts of revenge and their effects are still felt today.

V. *The Union League: Segregation through Terror.* Each carpetbag governor of each Southern state had his own private army, consisting of former slaves and black ex-Union soldiers. These militia forces protected the conquerors from Southern insurrections and from coup attempts by political rivals. These all-black armies laid waste to entire white towns and killed their former white masters, friends, and neighbours on the orders of governors.

The victimized whites never forgave the blacks for carrying out the orders of their Northern mercenary masters.

VI. *The Freedmen's Bureau: Segregation for Black Education.* The Bureau of Refugees, Freedmen, and Abandoned Lands, usually referred to as simply the Freedmen's Bureau, was the parent organization of the Union League. It represented the first unconstitutional foray by the federal government into education. The Freedmen's Bureau began the process of nationalizing Southern schools, building thousands of institutions, and paying for the construction through illegal activities. It focused on educating blacks, which included propagandizing for Republicans and hating "traitors" so that any hope of reconciliation with Southern whites was eradicated.

VII. *The Morrill Act: Segregating Whites for Re-Education.* During the early stages of the War for Southern Independence, a new federal agency was created: The Department of Agriculture. Then an unconstitutional education bill passed through Congress. It was called the Morrill Act. This nationalized schools both North and South.

The Department of Agriculture and the Morrill Act for agricultural and mechanical colleges came into being almost simultaneously. The Morrill Act donated 30,000 acres of federal land to the states for each representative in Congress for secondary schools. Both agencies have had a major impact on the American mind, especially in terms of separating the races.

Unknown to the American public, then and now, the seemingly innocuous Department of Agriculture conducted clandestine human behavior experiments related to special forms of educational curriculum. This was for Southern white children only. These experiments took place on Morrill land grant campuses.

VIII. *The Bureau of Education: Nationalizing Segregation.* From the fusion of land grants for secondary schools and agriculture experiments came their inevitable offspring: The Bureau of Education. This agency dominated most tax-supported schools in the United States. It spread the clandestine, radical, experimental forms of curriculum for whites to all public schools, North and South.

IX. *Segregation by Fusing Church and State.* In the antebellum South, religion bound blacks and whites together. Masters and slaves prayed and sang together, heard the same sermons at the same time. But during the war Northern Baptist, Methodist, and Presbyterian ministers poured into the South on the heels of the advancing Union armies. These zealous clerics often became the political leaders of the occupied South, the governors, congressmen, Union League and Freedmen's Bureau hierarchy.

Contrary to the Constitution, state and church merged via the army. After the war, white and black parishioners became segregated. The military confiscated Southern church property, then drove off or imprisoned the ministers and their white congregations. The army paid clergymen's salaries, funded new churches, wrote the sermons to conform to martial decrees and presidential policies, and made sure that only blacks attended these churches.

X. *Conclusion.* All these issues are not just about history and the past. They are directly related to today. Consider the following:

- Washington still blames Southern whites for being racists and conducts fraudulent witch-hunts to uncover them;
- As the covert physio-psychology experiments transformed into child-centered philosophy, it spread from Southern to Northern schools in the 20th century in the form of John Dewey's Progressivism. Predictably, test scores plummeted and illiteracy among students skyrocketed. This verified the accuracy of the original intention of emptying the minds of Southern children;

- Confiscation of Southern real property after the war has led to contemporary massive off-budget funding for many federal agencies. More sophisticated forms of seizure are now employed for the most trivial offenses;
- Segregation by force during Reconstruction led to desegregation by force in the 20th century; and
- More and more churches have become vehicles for spreading national policy, even when they are in direct conflict with a basic Christian worldview.

---

1 James Ronald Kennedy and Walter Donald Kennedy, *The South Was Right!* (Gretna, LA: Pelican Publishing Co., 1994), p. 19.

I. The Slave South: An Integrated Society

SOUTHERN SLAVE CULTURE was by necessity unsegregated. Slaves were involved in virtually every aspect of Southern economic life, both rural and urban. They were not only tillers of the soil but were represented in most skilled crafts. In the city of Charleston, about 27% of adult male slaves were skilled artisans. In several of the most important crafts of that city, including carpentry and masonry, slaves actually outnumbered whites. Some bondsmen even ascended into such professions as architecture and engineering.[2]

Slaves also held a large share of the skilled jobs in the countryside. On the large plantations, slaves predominated in the crafts and lower managerial ranks. To a surprising extent, slaves held top managerial posts as overseers or general managers. When acting as overseers, slaves were responsible not only for the overall direction of the labor force but for the scheduling of field operations and purchasing supplies.[3]

Frederick Law Olmsted, a Northern writer and Abolitionist, toured the South and found his ideas about the slave system changed: "In the selection of drivers [foremen] ... greater capacity of mind than the ordinary slave is often supposed to be possessed of, is certainly needed in them. A good driver is very valuable and usually holds the office for life. His authority is not limited to the direction of labor in the field, but extends to the general deportment of the negroes. He is made to do the duties of policemen, and even of police magistrate."[4]

About 7% of all slaves were managers within the agricultural sector. Some 11.9% were blacksmiths, carpenters, coopers, etc. Another 7.4% held semi-skilled or domestic jobs: teamsters, coachmen, gardeners, stewards, or servants. The common belief that all slaves were menial laborers is false.[5]

Contemporary Americans fail to recognize the existence of a flexible and effective system that operated within the framework of slavery. The notion that slave owners relied on the lash alone to promote discipline is a misleading myth.

To motivate slaves, planters used a wide range of rewards, including prizes for the individual or gang with the best picking record on a given day or during a given week. The prizes might be clothing, tobacco, whiskey, cash, or unscheduled holidays or trip to town on weekends. When slaves worked on their off days they received extra pay, often in cash in a pay rate prevailing for the hired laborer. Year-end bonuses, given in goods or cash, were frequently quite substantial. Bennett Barrow distributed gifts averaging $15 and $20 per slave family in both 1839 and 1840. The amounts received by particular slaves was proportional to their performance. A gift of $20 was about one-fifth of the national annual per capita income in 1840. A bonus of the same relative magnitude today would be about $1,000.

Slaves who worked well were rewarded with several acres of land. They grew their own crops in this land. The proceeds accrued to them. On the Texas plantation of Julian S. Devereux, slaves produced as much as two bales of cotton per patch. Devereux marketed their crop along with his own. In a good year slaves earned more than $100.[6]

Slave artisans hired out on their own account, operating in the same way as their free counterparts. They advertised their services, negotiated their own contracts, received money, paid debts themselves, obtained their own residences and places of business. A slave artisan, unlike his free counterpart, was required to pay a fixed percentage of his income to their masters. Some 31% of urban slave workers were on hire during 1860.[7]

Slaves could rise within their social and economic hierarchy. Field hands could become artisans or foreman. Artisans were allowed to move from the plantation to town where they could hire themselves out. Boys were apprenticed to carpenters, blacksmiths, or similar craftsmen when they were in their early teens, as was the case with whites.

There is too much evidence of deep personal attachments between owners and their bondsmen to deny that this was a facet of slave system. "Now my heart is nearly broke," wrote a Louisiana planter on the occasion of the death of his principal overseer. "I have lost poor Leven, one of the most faithful black men [that] ever lived. [He] was truth and honesty, and without a fault that I ever discovered. He has overseen the plantation nearly three years and done much better than any white man ever done here."[8]

To promote the stability of slave families, planters offered rewards, including such subsidies as separate housing for married couples, gifts of household goods, and cash bonuses. Marriage ceremonies were made solemn events by being performed in churches or in the big house. Marriages were accompanied by feasts and sometimes made occasions for a general holiday. While slave marriages were not provided for under the legal codes of the states, they were actively promoted under the plantation codes.

This points to a much-neglected feature of the legal structure of the antebellum South: within fairly wide limits the state turned codes of legal behavior of slaves over to the planters. Such duality of the legal structure was not unique to the antebellum South. It existed in medieval Europe in the duality between the law of the manor and of the Crown. It was characteristic of the regimes under which the American Colonies were governed.[9]

---

2 Robert W. Fogel and Stanley L. Engerman, *Time on the Cross* (New York: W.W. Norton & Company, 1974), p. 38

3 Ibid., pp. 39-40.

4 Frederick Law Olmsted, *Journeys and Explorations in the Cotton Kingdom of America* (New York: Mason Brothers, 1862), p. 249.

5 Fogel and Engerman, pp. 39-40.
6 *Ibid.*, p. 148.
7 *Ibid.*, p. 56
8 *Ibid.*, pp. 149, 77.
9 *Ibid.*, p. 128.

II. THE SLAVE SOUTH: AN INTEGRATED MILITARY

BLACK SOUTHERN SLAVES were in combat for the Confederacy long before Northern blacks. Although the Confederate government denied the legality of slave combatants until late 1864, under the principle of state sovereignty, each state and many private people made their own arrangements in relation to slaves as part of front-line forces.

Slaves found their way into the war in different ways. The largest number were servants. They had been cooks, butlers, carriage-drivers, and other skilled workers who had not worked in the fields but in the big house on plantations. An English observer estimated that there were 30,000 such men in the Army of Northern Virginia in 1862.[1]

A Union surgeon, caught behind Confederate lines in 1862, observed the Army of Northern Virginia moving toward Sharpsburg (Antietam) and marked in his diary on the presence of black Confederate soldiers:

> Wednesday, September 10. At 4 o'clock this morning the rebel army began to move from our town, Jacksons force taking the advance. The movement continued until 8 o'clock p.m., occupying 16 hours. The most liberal calculation could not give them 64,000 men. Over 3,000

Negroes must be included in that number ... They had arms, rifles, muskets sabers, bowie-knives, dirks, etc. They were supplied, in many instances, with knapsacks, haversacks, canteens, etc., and they were manifestly an integral portion of the Southern Confederacy army. They were seen riding on horses and mules, driving wagons, riding on caissons, in ambulances, with the staff of generals and promiscuously mixed up with the Rebel horde.[2]

The North's mistaken image of the black Southerner, that he could not possibly be expected to fight for the South, was used against them. A servant of Captain George Baylor of the 12th Virginia Cavalry Regiment lured an unsuspecting detachment of Yankees into a Confederate ambush, for example.[3]

One Confederate reported that when his regiment was into battle, their servants were in too, picking off Federal officers. During one charge, they found that a half dozen blacks had actually preceded them.[4]

In 1861 the 3rd Alabama Infantry Regiment marched to war with 1,000 white soldiers in the ranks and almost as many black men in the ranks as white.[5]

When one white Confederate refused to go forward with his company, at Mechanicsville, Va., a servant named Wesley came forward and asked permission to put on the deserter's accoutrements and take up his gun. He then went into action with the company, and though Minié balls of the enemy were falling thick and fast about them, Wesley never wavered, but brought down a Yankee at every fire.[6]

An old veteran remembered that his regiment's cooks would not remain in camp, but marched out with the rest, and fought behind their masters.[7]

John Parker was a slave who was pressed into service as an artilleryman at First Manassas. He had been a field hand on a large plantation. The master went off to war in 1861. Parker had been sent to work on the earthworks around Fredericksburg, Winchester, and Richmond. "I arrived at the junction two days before the action commenced," he recalled.

> They immediately placed me in one of the batteries. There were four colored men in our battery. I don't know how many there were in the others. We opened fire about 10 o'clock on the morning of Sunday the 21st; couldn't see the Yankees at all and only fired at random. Sometimes they were concealed in the woods and then we guessed our aim ... My work was to hand the balls and swab out the cannon; in this we took turns. The officers aimed the gun; we fired grapeshot. The balls from the Yankee guns fell quick around.[8]

Coleman Davis Smith was born in Virginia in 1844. He had been purchased by Lewis Davis and taken to Tennessee as a child. He was a playmate to the Davis children, including Sam Davis. As they grew into manhood, Sam and Coleman continued their close friendship: "Sam, David, and I worked together plowing and hoeing, doing such work as comes up on a farm. With the war, when Sam joined the army and became a soldier, Coleman went with him. And when Sam Davis became a spy, Coleman remembered that he and Sam scouted mostly. I remember we burned a wagon train of ammunition for the Yankees and more guns. We slept anywhere and ate anywhere."

The two stuck together; they were master and servant, but clearly also friends. When Sam was captured near Pulaski, Tenn., in 1863, so was Coleman. While Sam was charged as a spy, Coleman was not held. Northerners could not imagine the relationship between them, nor the role that Coleman played in the army or in Sam Davis's life. Although jailed with Sam at first, Coleman was released. While they were in jail together, Coleman begged Sam to tell the Yankees what they wanted to know, but Sam refused. After the execution of Sam Davis as a spy, Coleman Davis made his way back to the Davis farm near Smyrna.[9]

Black Southerners served in all branches of the Confederate armies. Black Tennessee military pensioners cited service in 40 different infantry units. They reported taking part in 35 separate engagements or campaigns, almost entirely in the Western Theater.[10]

1 Richard Rollins, editor, *Black Southerners in Gray: Essays on African-Americans in Confederate Armies* (Murfreesboro TN: Southern Heritage Press, 1994). p. 9.

2 Isaac W. Heysinger, *Antietam and the Maryland and Virginia Campaigns of 1862* (New York: Neale Publishing Co., 1912), pp. 122-123.

3 Wayne Austerman, "Virginia's Black Confederates," *Civil War Quarterly*, VIII, 1987, p. 42.

4 *Battlefields of the South* (New York: Johan Bradburn, 1865), pp. 157-158.

5 Rollins, p. 10.

6 *Battlefields of the South*, p. 284.

7 Rollins, p. 14.

8 James McPherson, *The Negro's Civil War* (Chicago: University of Illinois Press, 1982), pp. 22-23.

9 Rollins, p. 87.

10 *Ibid.*, p. 80.

III. PRESIDENTIAL RECONSTRUCTION: THE SOUTH STILL INTEGRATED

WITH ABRAHAM LINCOLN'S ASSASSINATION, Vice President Andrew Johnson assumed the highest political office. At first it seemed he would be a brutal tyrant over the shattered South. He said:

> For the thousands who were driven into the infernal rebellion there should be amnesty, conciliation, and mercy. For the leaders, justice. The penalty and the forfeit should be paid. The people must understand that treason is the blackest of crimes and must be punished.[1]

Johnson hated the slaveholding aristocrats with a bitter envy. "If Johnson was a snake," said a rival, Isham Harris, "he would lie in the grass and bite the heels of rich men's children. The very thought of an aristocrat caused him to emit venom and lash out in fury."[2]

Yet Andrew Johnson proved to be an insightful, moderate President. His policies promoted the same kind of mutually dependent, integrated Southern society that existed before the war. Now it was based on a modern employer/wage earner relationship.

Johnson's plan was restoration, bringing the South back into the Union in the shortest time, with the least amount of harsh military rule. This was not Reconstruction, which implied a long-term radical alteration of the minds, social framework, and economy of the South.

Johnson proclaimed amnesty for all except high-ranking military officers who left the United States to join the Confederacy and wealthy property owners, etc. He was devoted to the principle of state sovereignty. He believed most political matters should be left in the hands of the Southern states. Individual traitors should be punished but the states had never legally seceded or surrendered their rights to govern their own affairs.

As a result, for the first year after Appomattox the races were friendly. The freedmen received the best benefits of the old and new ways. They retained the lodgings and meals as under the slave system and received wages under the market system.

Johnson appointed provisional governors. He had to fill thousands of patronage jobs, which required picking many wartime Confederates. This brought rebels closer to real political power again. Johnson accepted this reality.

Andrew Johnson believed that Southerners were reasonable men who accepted the outcome of the war and the end of slavery. To convince the American public and Congress that his views were correct, he assigned special people to travel through the Southern states, to investigate the situation. He sent journalists Henry Watterson and Benjamin Truman, and also Ulysses S. Grant.

Watterson and Truman found that conditions justified Johnson's policies; the influential whites could be trusted to maintain loyal state governments. Grant found that Southerners were more peaceful than he expected.

Johnson then asked Carl Schurz to report on the South. Schurz was a Radical Republican and a militaristic German immigrant. His findings were very different. He wrote that Southern whites spent their time persecuting, beating, and killing Negroes and Unionists. Schurz and the radical newspapers reported comments made by idlers in barrooms and street corners and magnified them into the threatening voice of a whole people. Against these falsehoods, General Wager Swayne, the assistant commissioner for the Freedman's Bureau in Alabama in the early years of Reconstruction, said there had been no trouble from the Southern whites.

Black Codes Maintain Integrated South.

The Reconstruction-era Black Codes have been viewed as racist laws designed to re-enslave blacks. This is inaccurate. They were created under Andrew Johnson's presidency and reflect an attempt by both the Northern conquerors and the Southern employers to develop a stable work environment that would be fair to all sides. This was imperative in the face of the chaos, devastation, and poverty in the wake of total war.

The Black Codes Did Not Create Segregation.

They helped maintain the integrated society that existed before the war but now on a market-economy basis. The Black

Codes defined the freedmen's new rights and responsibilities. They gave the Negroes the right to own property, to sue and to be witness in court, where they could testify against whites. Labor contracts and apprentice laws were other aspects of the Black Codes.

Labor Contracts.

These were formulated by the Union Army. Wages were fixed by Northern judges. The carpetbag state governments enforced labor contracts, not Southern employers.

Apprentice Laws.

The war made orphans of thousands of children, white and black, and few people could look after them. Under slavery, no regulation of such things had been necessary. Now the children ran wild, in want and neglect, becoming criminals and vagabonds. Black fathers sometimes ran off when slavery ended, leaving their wives and children. The mothers were often unable to support their children. The apprentice laws made it possible to care for them. Children were apprenticed to suitable people. If the apprentice left without consent, he could be arrested and punished under the vagrancy laws. If the master was at fault, he could be fined, with the fine given to the apprentice. These measures were based on ordinary Northern vagrancy laws.

1 Walter L. Fleming, *Civil War and Reconstruction in Alabama* (New York: Columbia University Press, 1905), p. 347.

2 C.R. Hall, Andrew Johnson, *Military Governor of Tennessee* (Princeton: Princeton University Press, 1916), p. 22.

IV. Congressional Reconstruction: Segregation Begins

THADDEUS STEVENS was the radical Republican leader in the House of Representatives. Charles Sumner was the Radical head of the Senate and Ben Wade was the Radical president *pro tempore* of the Senate. They all loathed Andrew Johnson. They hated his moderate, conciliatory approach to healing the wounds of the war.

The Radicals had only limited success against the president's policies until external events shifted public sentiment away from reconciliation to retribution.

Bloody riots in New Orleans and Memphis left many blacks and Unionists dead or wounded. This allowed the Radicals to bring their harsh plans for the South to the foreground, even though former Northern soldiers were apparently among those fighting the blacks. Their plans would split the races apart forever and transform America permanently from a republic into a centralized dictatorship-in-progress.

To the Radicals the riots proved the South still seethed with the spirit of rebellion. But the New Orleans riot began as a result of inflammatory speeches by Republicans to fire up the freedmen to conduct destructive acts.

The Radical Republicans milked these incidents to ascend to political power: Horrors upon horrors accumulated, wrote a Louisiana carpetbagger to General Ben Butler as he related the gory details of how the rebel mayor, John C. Munro, armed his rebel police with revolvers and Bowie knives and privately ordered them to go and massacre the loyal men of New Orleans, adding that Andrew Johnson must be made responsible for this wholesale massacre and that it was Butler's job to rouse the Northern mind against this massacre.[1]

This letter forecast the Radical's program: revolutionary Reconstruction, no more moderate restoration; a complete overturn of the South's social, political, and economic existence. This meant viewing the ex-Confederacy as no longer part of the United States.

The radicals pursued two brutal principles, the state suicide and the conquered province theories, to prove that the South was an alien entity.

Charles Sumner formulated state suicide. The South by her actions had abdicated all constitutional rights. The Southern states had become territories under the exclusive control of Congress. Thus, there were no state governments in the South. They were now clean slates upon which Congress would write the laws. Congress alone would establish a republican form of government for them. This meant universal voting for "loyal" blacks and whites which in practice meant anyone who would vote Republican. This would nationalize voting qualifications. A republican form of government also meant universal education. This would expand Federal dominance over the minds of all citizens. The Radicals also proposed the ascendency of blacks over rebel whites to entrench the Republican Party. Since unqualified blacks would prevail in the Southern governments, a deep antagonistic wedge was driven between the races. This was segregation.

Thaddeus Stevens originated the conquered province theory. It was more extreme than the Summer plan. The law of war alone would rule the actions of Congress. The victors must treat the South as conquered provinces and settle them with Northern men and exterminate or drive out the present rebels as exiles from this country.[2]

Every inch of Southern soil should be confiscated for the costs of the war and for pensions to Union soldiers. For Stevens, secession had been successful. The South was out of the Union. The Constitution was torn to shreds. It was a bit of worthless parchment. The South must either come back as new states or remain as conquered provinces, with perpetual ascendency of the North and a Republican Congress. Democratic Representative Anthony Thornton of Illinois said that

> if the state which had seceded were out of the union, either in fact or in law, then the war has failed in its avowed object. If they are dead and defunct states, then the war was a fearful tragedy, resulting in the death of both the Union and the states. If they have lost their power of local government, then we have a despotism, a consolidated government, instead of one with specific limited powers.[3]

Stevens' more extreme views won out. He demanded and received approval from Congress to divide the South into military districts under a commander with absolute power and no timetable for the end of military rule.

The Radicals – 19th century Stalinists.

The fusing of a lawless dictatorship with Radical revolutionary philosophy produced the 19th century political equivalent of Stalinist collectivism. It was the moral precedent for the totalitarian horrors of the 20th century.

W.E.B. DuBois, the famed black Marxist historian, writing in the 1930s, when Stalinist redistribution was at its peak, saw the parallels between the conquered South and the vision of the Soviet Union. The Congressional Reconstruction laws created a dictatorship backed by the military arm of the United States by which the governments of the Southern states were to be coerced into accepting a new form of administration, in which the freedman and the putative poor whites were to hold the overwhelming balance of political power. As soon as the political power was successfully delivered into the hands of these elements, the federal government was to withdraw and full democracy ensue, with the State withering away, as Marx proclaimed: "Such dictatorship must last long enough really to put the mass of workers in power; that this would be in fact a dictatorship of the proletariat ..." [4] This was segregation by brute force.

DuBois then added:

And when the freedmen tried to imitate the manners of his brothers, and demanded real economic emancipation through ownership of land [re-distribution] and the right to use capital [of planters' money], there arose the bitter shriek of property and the charge of corruption, and theft was added to that of ignorance and poverty, just as we have seen in our day in the case of Russia.[5]

The Civil Rights Bill: Military Rule Splits Races.

On March 2, 1867, the Civil Rights Bill passed Congress. President Johnson vetoed it, but it passed over his veto.

The bill declared that Southern civil governments were not legal unless controlled by the military and Congress. Military commanders could appoint or remove civil officers. It turned the South into a Marxist-type dictatorship and separated the races permanently.

President Johnson gave these reasons for his veto:

> It intervenes between capital and labor and attempts to settle questions of political economy through the agency of numerous officials, whose interest it will be to ferment discord between the races; for as the breach widens, their employment will continue, and when it is closed their occupation will end, Johnson declared that this law establishes for the security of the colored race safeguards which go infinitely beyond any that the General Government has ever provided for the

white race, and therefore discriminates against the white race.[6]

The 14th Amendment: National Justice Splits Races.

This amendment to the Constitution built on the principles of the Civil Rights Act, Section One, provided that all persons born or naturalized in the United States are citizens of the United States. (Formerly they had been citizens of their own states.) This section destroyed the Bill of Rights' restrictions on Federal power and has been used extensively by the Supreme Court to undermine the validity of state legislation and to draw almost every facet of life beneath federal jurisdiction.

Section Three excluded from political office those army officers and members of Congress who aided the Confederacy. By implication this allowed unqualified freedmen to fill these places, creating a bitter rift between blacks and whites.

The 14th Amendment Ratified Over Citizens' Veto.

President Johnson, noting that only 25 of the 36 states were represented in Congress, questioned the legality of the amendment. Every Southern state voted against it. This prompted Senator James Doolittle of Wisconsin to say: "The people of the South have rejected the constitutional amendment and we will march on them and force them to adopt it at the point of a bayonet.[7]

When the South was threatened with not being re-admitted into the Union unless they ratified, ten states accepted it.

The 15th Amendment: Nationalized Votes, Alienates Races.

This amendment turned the classic social order upside-down. Voting qualifications were set in Washington, not each state, as mandated by the Constitution. Freedmen became the dominant voter class while most whites were disqualified. The blacks adhered to the carpetbaggers, who passed laws against their former white masters, neighbors, and friends. This was segregation, the political alienation of the races.

Yet even in Congress, the Radical Committee of Fifteen which had convened to give the vote to Southern blacks, had questions about the validity of their actions. Doubts were entertained whether Congress had the power, even under the amended Constitution, to prescribe the qualifications of voters in a state, or if could it act directly on the subject: "It is doubtful, in the opinion of your committee, whether states would consent to surrender a power they had always exercised."[8]

In March 1870, the 15th Amendment was ratified.

The Consequences of Congressional Reconstruction.

In August 1870 Robert E. Lee met with former Confederate leaders. He is said to have told Fletcher Stockdale, the war-time Governor of Texas: "Governor, if I had foreseen the use these people [Republicans] designed to make of their victory, there would have been no surrender at Appomattox Courthouse; no sir, not by me. Had I foreseen the results of subjugation, I would have preferred to die at Appomattox with my brave men, my sword in this right hand."9

Jabez Curry, a Confederate congressman and cavalry officer, described the permanent, negative changes in the United States government as a result of Congressional Reconstruction:

> The Constitution is wiped out. Grants have no significance. Limitations are impotent. Instead of stable, solemn, permanent national will, we have hardly a rope of sand, and the Constitution, as Jefferson feared, became "waste paper."10

Congressional Reconstruction begot racial hatred and segregation. A former abolitionist reporter, from Maine, wrote:

> The carpetbaggers went to the colored people and said, "we are your friends" and all that sort of thing. They got their confidence and control. The [Southern] white people did not go among them. The colored people in that way were made inimical to the white people, and led to think that their interests were antagonistic to the interests of the white people. The white people held the property and what little money there was. The colored people were taught by these men [the carpetbaggers] to believe that the lands properly belonged to them and not to their former masters; that the dwelling houses and the gin houses, and everything else, belonged to them. I heard that stated on the stump last summer ... Senator Beverly Nash, a colored man, at Columbia, a very shrewd, sharp, keen man, in a public speech to

6,000 or 8,000 men, said to them, "The reformers complain of taxes being too high. I tell you they are not high enough. I want them taxed until they put these lands back to where they belong, into the hands of those who worked them. You toiled for them, and were sold to pay for them and you ought to have them. It was a fierce contest from beginning to end, to array race against race.[11]

This antagonism has continued to the present day.

---

1 William Hesseltine, *Ulysses S. Grant, Politician* (New York: Frederick Unger Publishing Co., 1957), p. 70.

2 Fleming, p. 340.

3 *Congressional Globe*, 39th Congress, First Session (Washington, D.C.: Reprint edition by United States Historical Documents Institute, Inc., 1970), p. 1165.

4 W.E.B. Dubois, *Black Reconstruction in America* (New York: S.A Russell Co., 1935), p. 345.

5 *Ibid.*, p. 206.

6 *Ibid.*, p. 282.

7 *Southern Patriot*, November-December 1999, p. 3

8 DuBois, p. 312.

9 Thomas Cary Johnson, *The Life and Letters of Robert Lewis Dabney* (Richmond: The Presbyterian Committee of Publication, 1903), pp. 499-500.

10 Jabez L.M. Curry, *Principles, Acts and Utterances of John C. Calhoun, Promotive of the True Union of the States* (Chicago: University of Chicago Press, 1898), p. 25.

11 James S. Pike, *The Prostrate State* (New York: Loring and Mussey, 1935), p. 222.

V. THE UNION LEAGUE: SEGREGATION THROUGH TERROR

CONGRESSIONAL RECONSTRUCTION was the opening wedge that pried apart whites and blacks. Then came the Union League. Alienation of the races became open war that was so bitter that its aftertaste resulted in their permanent separation.

The Union League began as a political club in New York in 1863 to revive the sagging patriotic spirits of the Northern states during the War for Southern Independence. Its philosophies were similar to the Radical Republicans, so it fused with and became part of Republican vote-building machine for blacks in the post-war South.

The Union League's Private Black Armies

Northern army officers, religious leaders, and other assorted carpetbaggers became the governors of the defeated Southern states. They achieved these exalted positions through military force, fraudulent elections, and vote-getting through terror. Other carpetbaggers, desiring the spoils of these positions, realized that only greater violence could turn out the incumbents. So, both the leading politicians and their rivals hired private armies, composed of black Union League men, to overcome their adversaries. This meant that Southern blacks were aiding the enemies of the South to maintain alien rulers to keep their white neighbors down.

The Union League's expenses were covered by the sale of confiscated white Southerners' property, thus inciting the volunteers to harass the people in time of peace by unlawful seizure to provide the means of paying themselves.[1] This further alienated whites from blacks.

In North Carolina, Governor William W. Holden boasted of the magnitude of his black Union League militia forces: "I can control at my word, 80,000 men."[2] Holden was the head of the Union League in the state.

In South Carolina, Governor Robert Scott armed 20,000 Negro militiamen to support his election in 1870. Altogether there were a quarter-million black Union League troops in the South.

In Arkansas, these militiamen produced the famous Brooks-Baxter War. In the 1872 gubernatorial election two corrupt Republican candidates, Joseph Brooks and Elisha Baxter, fought each other. There were many irregularities in the voting. Brooks was declared the winner but Baxter took possession of the office. Brooks's black militia showed Baxter out of the State House. Baxter set up his own government and called up his militia. There was much firing between the two groups of Republican black militias. Then President Grant recognized Baxter. The war was over.

In 1868 in Louisiana Henry Clay Warmoth, a former Union Army officer, was elected Republican governor. He became a millionaire. In 1871 Warmoth was opposed by Republicans Stephen B Packard, a U.S. Marshal, and George Carter, speaker of the Louisiana House. The office was just too temptingly lucrative. When the legislature convened, Carter was expelled. A Warmoth man was installed as speaker. Carter set up a second legislature. Warmouth called up 5,000 militia and attacked Carter. Carter's militia counter-attacked the State House and failed. President Grant ordered Federal troops against Carter. His men returned Warmoth to the State House.

Election day, 1872: Warmoth was now opposed by Packard, John McEnery, and William P. Kellogg. There were two election boards and two winners: Kellogg and McEnery. Packard set up his own government. The legislators impeached Warmoth. Kellogg was declared the winner. Warmoth set up his own government. Lt. Governor P.B.S. Pinchback, a Negro, called up the black militia against Warmoth. McEnery's militia attacked police headquarters. It was repulsed.

1874: The Republican black militias of Kellogg and McEnery fought a pitched battle. Kellogg's men surrendered. President Grant ordered in Federal troops. Kellogg was put into the State House. 1876: Again, two governors as both Packard and the Democrat Francis Nichols claimed victory. Packard seized the State House. Then Rutherford B. Hayes was elected president. All Federal troops were withdrawn from the South. Packard left the state with the reward of ambassador to Britain.

In Mississippi's 1875 election, James Alcorn, a former governor, faced Radical Governor Adelbert Ames. Under Ames, the Union League increased. He said that since the state government "commands respect of the colored race only, it must depend for military support on colored troops."[3]

During the campaign Alcorn denounced a Radical sheriff named Brown. Brown assembled his black militia, provoking a battle at Friar's Point, Alcorn's home town. When the smoke cleared, Brown's militia was in retreat. Ames responded by calling up his Union League militia. United States Attorney General Edwards Pierrepont negotiated a settlement. All three sides disbanded their militias. Without the corrupt Republican carpetbagger private armies, the Democrats easily took the legislature. They planned to impeach Ames, but he resigned first.

In Texas in 1873 Governor Edmund Davis was defeated by Judge Richard Coke. Davis used his Union League militia to retake the Austin State House. When President Grant refused to send federal troops, Davis capitulated.

Black Militia Terrorize Whites.

The Union League militia also harassed and bullied and sometimes murdered Southern whites, greatly increasing the trend toward segregation.

In South Carolina, Joe Crew, a militia captain, told his men that if they wanted provisions they should take what they wanted. If the whites objected, they should burn down their homes.

Senator Francis Blair of Missouri spoke of the following case:

> The colored militia were on parade [in Union, S.C.] with arms in their hands. They met on the

road a one-armed white man who had formerly been in the Confederate service. He had whiskey in his wagon. This they demanded, flourishing their arms. He gave them some. Then they demanded more. This he declined, upon the ground that it was not his property .... They deliberately took him from his wagon, carrying him into the woods, and there shot him in cold blood .... To permit such a case to go unpunished ... would be the equivalent to the granting of a roving commission of theft and blood.[4]

Barn burning was the most common crime committed by the black Union League militia against whites. The loss of a barn could mean complete ruin to a farmer. North Carolina State Senator John Stephens, at a Union League meeting, gave matches to the blacks, saying they would be useful in burning out the white people: nine barns burned in one night, along with a hotel, a row of houses, and the tobacco crops of leading citizens. Stephens was later executed by the Ku Klux Klan. His death provoked the anti-Klan law of 1870. Governor Holden could then declare any county to be in insurrection and send in the Union League militia, which was led by Colonel George "Cut Throat" Kirk. He marched through Caswell and Alamance counties. They were alleged to be in insurrection. Kirk committed atrocities which the *New York World* denounced as a disgrace to the 19th century.[5]

In Arkansas, two days before the 1868 general election, Governor Powell Clayton declared martial law. Then came four months of terrorism. White townspeople fled the black militia, who roamed the country, torturing and killing those they captured. Towns like Warren and Hamburg were gutted. The prisoner was "killed while attempting to escape" was a familiar phrase in the militia commander's reports.[6]

In Georgia, during the election of 1868, there was a march of 300 heavily armed Union League blacks from Albany to Camilla, led by two white Republican leaders, for a rally. The sheriff at Camilla urged them to disband. They refused. He gathered a posse. Both sides opened fire. Thirty-two Union League blacks were casualties.

The Union League presented this as a massacre, in which heartless whites butchered helpless Negroes. Yet even the carpetbag investigation found the violence was caused by the Union League's march.

In 1870 a Congressional committee investigated a secret terror organization called the Ku Klux Klan. Supposedly it violently abused blacks and intended to reinstate slavery. Yet this committee found that the Klan arose as a result of the Union League's brutality and that the Klan was falsely charged with crimes to generate more power for the carpetbaggers and divert attention away from their enormous corruption. According to author Stanley Horn, in his 1969 work *The Invisible Empire: The Story of the Ku Klux Klan, 1866-1871*,

> Had there been no wanton oppression in the South, there would have been no Ku Kluxism. Had there been no rule of the tyrannical, corrupt carpetbaggers or Scalawags, there would have been no secret organizations.[7]

The Consequences of the Union League for Today.

"The prejudices and antagonisms that the Union League fostered are felt to this day. It is obvious that if the positive tendencies of the days following the war had been cultivated and allowed to take their course, the problems of the Negro freedman would have slowly evolved a solution. By and large, the white leaders of Georgia were sincerely and seriously interested in the welfare of the Negro," wrote Georgia historian Roberta Cason. "[The Union League] did more to breed suspicion between the races, to create misunderstandings, to ignite often justifiable but nonetheless dangerous explosions of feeling and conduct, to estrange the black man from the people among whom he must live, to fan alive and to kindle in new places fires of prejudice, than any other single influence." [8]

---

1 *Congressional Globe*, 40th Congress, Second Session, p. 510.

2 Stanley Horn, *The Invisible Empire: The Story of the Ku Klux Klan, 1866-1871* (Cos Cob, CT: John E. Edwards, 1969), p. 17.

3 James Garner, *Reconstruction in Mississippi* (New York: The MacMillan Co., 1901), p. 385.

4 Francis P. Blair, "Protection of Life in the South," speech in the United States Senate, April 3-4, 1871 (Washington D.C.: F. and J. Rives and George A. Bailey, 1871), p. 14.

5 Horn, p. 199.

6 *Ibid.*, p. 260.

7 *Ibid.*, p. 2.

8 Roberta Cason, "The Union League in Georgia," *Georgia Historical Quarterly*, vol. 20 (1936), p. 153.

VI. THE FREEDMEN'S BUREAU: SEGREGATION FOR BLACK EDUCATION

THE UNION LEAGUE, for all its destructiveness for race relations, was only a division of a larger organization – the Freedmen's Bureau. It was an agency of the War Department. Its role in the post-war South was enormous and its educational projects that were put in place in the 1860s became national models for the 20th century. Its political directives for the special treatment of blacks and the hunting down of racists is still expanding in the contemporary United States and continues to impact current national policy.

The Union League separated blacks from whites by violence. This was a short-term measure. The Freedmen's Bureau transformed the minds of blacks and whites permanently through different forms of special education. This laid a foundation for the eternal segregation of the races.

Education became re-education, in its varied forms. Education for literacy and politically correct voting, for blacks. Education outside the classroom to erase the culture of rebellion for whites.

Its complete title, The Bureau of Refugees, Freedmen, and Abandoned Lands, shows the full extent of its jurisdiction. It controlled the four million blacks who had been slaves. It controlled the destiny of white refugees displaced by the war and confiscated tens of millions of acres of property abandoned by the "traitors."

Re-education for reactionary whites was not achieved within the schoolhouse but through sophisticated mind-control techniques. These included crop control and relocation.

The primary function of the Freedmen's Bureau was educating blacks to vote Republican and to forever hate Southern whites. Integration was unthinkable, except in some rare showcase schools, where it was used to torment whites with radical principles of social equality.

Major General Oliver Otis Howard was Commissioner of the Freedmen's Bureau. He was a hardened veteran who had been through some of the worst carnage of the war. During the near-annihilation of the Union Army in the Peninsula Campaign, Howard's right arm was blown off. This forever embittered him toward the South.

Bureau Law Over Civil Law.

On April 2, 1866, President Andrew Johnson proclaimed that the war was over. Civil law would resume. Oliver Otis Howard countered with his view that this did not remove martial law or operate in any way upon the Freedmen's Bureau in the exercise of its jurisdiction.

By means of the Bureau courts, the Negro was completely removed from trial by civil government and any of its officers, except when the latter were acting as Bureau agents. As Walter

L. Fleming wrote in his 1905 work, *Civil War and Reconstruction in Alabama,* an Army officer and two or three carpetbaggers administered what they called justice.[1]

Civil officers were gradually replaced by Bureau men. Thus, the state government passed into the hands of the Bureau.[2]

President Johnson called General Howard a fanatic.[3] By fusing the civil and the military power, the Bureau became a centralized dictatorship. Here Howard describes the consequences of his enormous despotic power: "Almost unlimited authority gave me scope and liberty of action ... Legislative, judicial, and executive powers were combined in my commission."[4]

Andrew Johnson pointed out the meaning of such unlimited scope of action against civilians:

> The power thus given to the commanding officer over all the people ... is that of an absolute monarch ... He alone is permitted to determine the rights of persons and property ... It places at his free disposal all the lands and goods in his district, and he may distribute them without let or hindrance to whom he pleases. Being bound by no State law, and there being no other law to regulate the subject, he may make a criminal code of his own; and can make it as bloody as any in history ... Everything is a crime which he chooses to call so, and all persons are condemned who he pronounces to be guilty. [5]

By 1869 some 2,228 schools were in operation, teaching 114,522 pupils, mainly blacks.

Segregating Blacks to Vote Republican.

James P. Wickersham was a Radical Republican educator and politician. Here he describes the necessity of educating blacks apart from the whites to insure they vote correctly, since they were largely the only voting class:

> What can Education do for the freedmen? Four millions of human beings have been emancipated in the South. They are now without property, without that knowledge and those habits of self-reliance and self-direction. They are ignorant, simple hearted and superstitious ... Let teachers and missionaries be sent to them. Let State and Church and neighborhoods unite in a grand effort to save them from destruction. We all know that the freedmen must be educated. We all know that the education that they need is not merely to read and write ... but as well to fight for their new condition as freedmen and citizens .... A loaded musket in the hands of a crazy man in a crowd is not as dangerous as a ballot in the hands of an ignorant man at an election.[6]

Black Education for Revolution, Hate, Segregation.

Revered Buckley, the Freedmen's Bureau superintendent of education in Alabama, reported as late as March 15, 1867, that native whites favored black education and no difficulty was experienced in getting Southern whites to support Negro schools. But, as Fleming wrote, too many Bureau teachers

> considered themselves missionaries whose duty it was to show the southern people the error of their sinful ways, and who taught the negro the wildest of social, political, and religious doctrines ... The negro was taught by the missionary educator that he must distrust the whites and give up all habits and customs that would remind him of his former condition; he must not say "master" or "mistress," nor take his hat off when speaking to a white person. In teaching him not to be servile, they taught him to be insolent. The missionary teachers regarded themselves as the advance guard of a new army of invasion against the terrible South.[7]

Thus, the burning of schoolhouses was not a racist act nor from a fear of teaching blacks. Schools were burned because they became meeting places for the Bureau and the Union League, where revolutionary and violent acts were planned.

Relocation as Re-education for Whites.

Southern whites were mostly to be re-educated by the Bureau outside of the classroom. This is one way they were to learn the new social order:

> Cairo, Illinois ... Serve[d] as a portal through which thousands of poor whites ... were sent into the loyal states ... Many of these became permanent residents ... [Those who refused to

work] were kept under military surveillance and guided authoritatively toward some definite means of self-support ... The educational influence of the change was noticeable and most important .... Returning South, after perhaps a year's absence, to the neighborhood of their former homes ... transformation through living in the midst of industries of the North was really very great. They had made the discovery that the possession of a vast property in the ownership of slaves ... was not essential either to self-respect or social standing.[8]

This phase of the Reconstruction of the South did not affect many people and could not be called a success.

Crop Control as Re-education.

Whites were also to be re-educated outside the classroom in other sophisticated ways. Congress saw in the word "cotton" the living metaphor for why the war began and why the spirit of rebellion would not be extinguished. Cotton endlessly reminded Southerners of ideas that supposedly had driven them to secede: slave labor, state sovereignty, restrictions on governmental power, and free trade. These views had been repudiated as the post-war United States became a centralized protectionist world power. Thus, cotton would have to be diffused among new crops, to end those old, reactionary perspectives. According to the 1866 Annual Report of the Commissioner of Agriculture

In the reorganization of the Southern states, it is believed that the great mistake of the past, the concentration of labor mainly upon a single branch of a single grand division of productive industry, will be avoided ... Diversification must be applied to a reorganized Southern agriculture ... Cotton will never again overshadow and dwarf other interests essential to permanent success in agriculture.[9]

Nationalizing Bureau Schools for Permanence.

Initially, following the war, religious and secular aid groups competed with the Freedmen's Bureau for the ex-slaves' education until 1866, when Congress appropriated funds to the Bureau for school construction. Then Bureau programs assumed a permanent character. Private agencies were required to comply with its bureaucratic standards. This centralized all education within the Bureau.

In his autobiography, General O.O. Howard described his plan to permanently consolidate all Southern schools. This would be the prelude to nationalizing them. "I wished to stimulate every educational interest till our government schools and those of benevolent societies should become absorbed in a great free system."[10]

Radical Republicans like Howard, who hated the South, claimed that white Southerners were illiterate and would not support tax-funded schools. Radicals believed that only federalizing all their schools would alter this situation. But there was an unstated reality behind these claims: The state

(Alabama) was bankrupt, Walter Fleming wrote in *Civil War and Reconstruction in Alabama.*

> Carpetbaggers took all the state income for one last chance at spoils. No money for schools. Most Negro and many white schools closed. Teachers, when paid at all by the state, were paid in depreciated state scrip for education. Year-by-year an increasing amount was diverted to other uses.[11]

---

1 Fleming, p. 439.

2 *Ibid.*, p. 426.

3 *Cincinnati Gazette*, August 23, 1867.

4 *Annual Report of the Secretary of War for the Year 1869* (Government Printing Office), pp. 499, 504.

5 Andrew Johnson, "Veto of First Reconstruction Act," March 2, 1867.

6 J.P. Wickersham, *Education as an Element in the Reconstruction of the Union* (Boston: C.C. Rand and Avery, 1865), p. 8.

7 Fleming, p. 465.

8 John Eaton, *Grant, Lincoln, and the Freedmen* (New York: St. Martin's Press, 1930), p. 37

9 *Annual Report of the Commissioner of Agriculture for the Year 1866*, p. 6.

10 Oliver O. Howard, *Autobiography of Oliver Otis Howard, Major General, United States Army* (New York: Baker and Taylor, 1907), p. 358.

11 Fleming, p. 631.

VII. THE MORRILL ACT: SEGREGATING WHITES FOR RE-EDUCATION

THE FREEDMEN'S BUREAU CREATED a huge system of schools for blacks, to insure they would become Republican voters and hate Southern whites.

The white children of the ex-Confederacy also needed to be educated in the classroom. After all, they were the offspring of traitors and rebels. Their re-education was a high priority. For the Radical Republicans, education would be the instrument for reforming the Southern mind to be sympathetic to the principles of union and liberty, and for training Southerners to be obedient to Republican Party rule. In a sense, the school was the common denominator, the agency for nationalization of the sectionally minded South. Some Radical Republicans saw secession as having developed from wide-spread illiteracy and social stratification in the South. So, education became to the Reconstructionists a way of remaking the South in the Republican Image.

During the War for Southern Independence, this Radical viewpoint took legislative form. Congress created the Morrill Act, to fund colleges from federal lands in each state; and a Department of Agriculture, for crop research. These seemingly unconnected entities would eventually fuse their objectives into a research project for a revolutionary, mind-altering curriculum, exclusively for Southern whites. This meant that whites and blacks must be kept apart.

The Morrill Act and War.

By 1862 the Union Army had suffered major military reverses and Robert E. Lee was maneuvering to bring the war to the North. The Republicans were not sure they could win.

In such a desperate atmosphere, the Morrill Act passed Congress. In the peace time of 1857 it had failed. Now it gave the federal government powers over the states that it never had before.

The Morrill Act's stated objective was to fund colleges to teach agriculture and mechanic arts. Washington donated 30,000 acres of federal land to each state for each representative in Congress.

When Representative Justin Morrill of Vermont first introduced his education bill in 1857, it passed Congress but President James Buchanan vetoed it, saying: "Should the time ever arrive when the state governments shall look to the Federal treasury for the means of supporting themselves and maintaining their systems of educational and internal policy, the character of both governments will be greatly deteriorated."[1]

It should be noted that Morrill also gave his name to the Morrill Tariff of 1861, which lavished profits on Northern industrialists at the expense of agriculturalists.

In Congress, there were also strenuous objections to the Morrill Act. Senator George E. Pugh of Ohio said:

> It is just as much a violation of our duty to invade the province of our state governments under the head of donations as it would be to invade them by force and violence. If you proceed to a detailed examination of the bill, you will see that its object is entirely to displace the control of the state governments over the most important of all the pursuits of our citizens ... and the federal government as forever to supersede them and install us.[2]

Then the War for Southern Independence began. And with it, the withdrawal of the Southern Democrats from Congress. They had blocked federal expansion by voting against Morrill. With their absence Morrill easily became law. All the immense state higher education systems of the 20th century have been built on Morrill land.

The legislative language of the Morrill Act disguised its intention. It was not only an education bill but also a research bill. Morrill funded a national education system to provide scientists for military research, including weapons development: courses of study bearing on the application of science to military pursuits and pedagogical research for post-war stability in the South.

The military research led to advances in repeating rifles, ironclad warships, artillery barrels improved for greater accuracy, the modern jacketed bullet, etc.

Later amendments designated each Morrill campus as a military base. For years after peace returned to the South, a quarter-million Union troops and militiamen occupied the ex-Confederacy, defending the carpetbagger governments. But these alien rulers were gradually pushed out, along with their armed forces. The federal government desperately needed to maintain a low-profile military presence in the South.

This was achieved through the Morrill colleges. One amendment stated that each student was required to take a course in military tactics. Another read: "Ordnance is to be stockpiled in each land-grant college. An officer from the Army and the navy is to be part of the staff, to be a superintendent or professor."[3] Still another amendment increased the number of officers on each campus to 85. Separate barracks, a separate armory and separate facilities were provided for officers at the schools.[4] Later, military superintendents at each of the schools were required to make quarterly reports to the adjutant-general of the army. This put the War Department directly into the business of overseeing the campuses. Finally, military study obligates the student to volunteer for military duty.[5] The Morrill campuses were on a war footing.

The Hatch Act as "Seven Days in May."

After the war, pedagogical research replaced martial research. This accelerated in 1887 when a major amendment to Morrill Act passed Congress. It was called the Hatch Act. It seemed harmless enough to provide funding for agricultural experiment stations, apparently to improve the dairy industry, animal breeding, and crops. The Hatch Act centralized the direction of the research away from the states into Washington. It fused Agriculture Department research with Morrill research.

The Agriculture Department's Commissioner in the late 1880s called for still more centralization:

> For many years it had become more and more apparent that one great need of the agricultural interests of the United States, is a better understanding and a more intimate relation between the several agricultural colleges and experiment stations and the Department of Agriculture, to develop systems which should better unify results of experiments and reports upon them. These agricultural colleges were severally endowed by the one-the-same act of Congress. They are now separately carrying on experiments at an expense of the time and means, and yet without any central head through which to report and compare results with each other .... No suitable provision has been made by the national government for any extended practical experiments in this direction .... The Department of Agriculture can, if wisely conducted, become a vigorous center for a more cooperative effort for the promotion of agricultural science.[6]

In reality, the underlying significance of the Hatch Act was to create, under Washington's control, a covert laboratory environment, where scientists could develop, without the outer world's knowledge, a revolutionary and radical kind of curriculum. It would be only for the whites of the South, to reeducate them and to destroy their culture and memories of their past. This new curriculum would alter the mentality of the children of the ex-Confederacy, so they would not share their parents' worldview and never follow another Robert E. Lee.

The methods by which the program was developed is reminiscent of the motion picture, *Seven Days in May*. In that film, a general's aide (Kirk Douglas) discovers the existence of the secret military base in a desolate area, where no such base is authorized. Gradually it becomes evident that the troops there are preparing for a coup against the president. This operation remained undetected because the military's obsession with deceptive code names to compel secrecy fooled the congressional watchdogs.

The Hatch Act's history is similar to the movie. The agricultural experiment stations were located in remote, hidden sites, far from outsiders' prying eyes. Its evasive legislative title (Agricultural Experiment Stations) confused Southerners as to its intention. It could only apply to curriculum, students, and education by twisting the logic of Darwinian evolution theory.

Via Darwin's vision, man was the highest rung in the general animal kingdom and shared many of the physical characteristics of the lower life forms. From that perspective agriculture experiments meant studies based on comparative anatomy. By using the findings of how a horse or a cow or a chicken's brain or nervous system absorbs or transmits information, revolutionary educational materials could be developed, based solely on physiology. This included how animals mature and the biological sequence of their ability to assimilate data.

This was a completely at odds with tradition, which fused religion, cultural values, and a powerful sense of loyalty to one's community to create the basic ingredients of education. But from Washington's perspective, these were the elements that had produced the fanatical traitors who refused to submit to national authority. Education through physiology bypassed the cultural factors that had generated these opponents of centralized government.

The new curriculum materials would be presented to Southern white children in a specific sequence based on their neurological or biological maturity. Those materials that stimulated a strong electrical flow of the brain or induced a more rapid heart-beat were used. In this context, interest meant this physiological stimulation, not emotional enthusiasm, which could not be measured. If it could not be measure by a voltmeter it was meaningless. This was Behaviorism. "The laws which express the development and activity of the nervous mechanism must determine pedagogical principles," wrote the Commissioner of the Bureau of Education.

> The application of the comparative method [animal to human study] has led the investigator to the mental manifestations of the lower animals. ... We are devoting a good deal of attention to the study of children. ... From the first we had a little experiment school ... It has the same relation to

the education department that an experiment farm would have to the department of agriculture.[7]

Stanley Hall, one of the pioneers in physiological education, identified the change in education as early as the 1890s:

> A score of psycho-physic laboratories, with more men and apparatus than can be found in all of Europe combined, are now in operation. A glance at the chief fields now cultivated by a complete university department of psychology, will show how transforming for other philosophical disciplines, how all conditioning for education, how full of promise for religion, this regenerate 'science of man' is now fast becoming. Studies focus on: senses, motion, time of psychic action, fatigue, pain, perception, association, attention. They shed new light on many old corners and they have already reconstructed many old doctrines. Experiments are made of muscle groups with drugs, heat, light, sound. It has little ethical power in it, hence few psychologists have the strength to go on. It is 'psychology without soul.' Another field is comparative psychology. The more we know of animal life, the vaster becomes our conception of instinct.[8]

What prevented this New Psychology, as it was called, from adhering to education, was that it lacked a philosophy. It was too cut and dry. It required a new generation of psychologists and pedagogues to bridge the gap. This was personified by John Dewey. He turned the abstract principles of psychological comparative anatomy into the educational curriculum ideals of the 20th century. And this erased American culture, not only in the South but the North, as well.

Dewey's philosophy was called Progressivism. This was child-centered education, the inescapable outcome of physiology as the basis of curriculum. The student's interests were paramount. The teacher, the school, the curriculum, was geared to developing the feelings, thoughts, and creative sparks that the student manifested. Societal heritage, cultural, and external values were forcibly discarded. Via Dewey's ideas of evolution, knowing was entirely physiological. Like the historical development of a species, each child evolved at its own physical rate. Curriculum was geared to reflect each new stage of growth. And unlike the supposedly bad authoritarian past, where children sat quietly for hours, physical movement for exploration was encouraged, as if they were restless animals.

Because Progressivism was based on the empirical model, where subjective experience, in scientific experiments, was the basis, change was an inherent factor. In scientific experiments, altering one factor, like adding two centimeters of sulfuric acid instead of one, produces a change in the observed reaction. This is an excellent method for analyzing the properties of an inert substance. It is disastrous when applied to children because teaching for change means teaching only for now. There can be no future because everything will be different tomorrow. This required that all truths must be tentative. This meant that the child would learn no values or ideals worth believing in, fighting for, or dying for. This would eliminate the intellectual and cultural through-line of now to the future. It would take away the thought of abstract concepts about what does not exist now, like the moral consequences of our actions.

---

1 *Congressional Globe*, 35th Congress, Second Session, p. 1412.

2 *Congressional Globe*, 35th Congress, Second Session, p. 714.

3 *Annual Report of the Commissioner of the Bureau of Education, for the Year 1890*, pp. 626-27.

4 *Ibid.*, pp. 627 and 630.

5 *Ibid.*, pp. 630-31.

6 *Annual Report of the Commissioner of Agriculture for the Year 1885*, pp. 6- 7.

7 *Annual Report of the Commissioner of the Bureau of Education for the Year 1894*, p. 360.

8 *Ibid.*, p. 445.

VIII. The Bureau of Education: Nationalizing Segregation

IN 1867, A SMALL AGENCY was created by Congress. It was called the Bureau of Education. It consisted of only five employees: a supervisor and four clerks, "to collect such statistics and facts as shall show the condition and progress of education in the several states and territories ... as shall aid the people of the United States in the establishment and maintenance of efficient school systems, and otherwise promote the cause of education throughout the country."[1]

From this miniscule beginning, over time, the Bureau of Education became a gigantic department, nationalizing, controlling, and separating black and white primary and secondary schools by administering the Morrill colleges and absorbing the Freedmen's Bureau schools into its own bureaucracy.

From its inception it was obvious that the desire to destroy the minds of Southern whites was behind this new agency. U.S. Representative George F. Hoar of Massachusetts stated:

> I ask the attention of the House to the following letter from a distinguished lawyer in Tennessee, giving an account of the school system in the state: "The law as it now stands in our state, carefully and zealously provides for the barbarism and debasement of posterity. ... It prefers that the

masses grow up prejudiced and ignorant and brutal. Narrow-minded and provincial itself, it anxiously desires to have the community which suffers from its depraved teachings still more illiterate, if possible, than itself. Its blighting influence would soon come to an end if provision was once fully made that the rising generation should be educated. Like all other vicious despotisms, it fears and dreads the enlightenment of the people. ... I can only say that unless the General government will act, I can see but little prospect being done in our state during the present generation, at least." The history of the last ten years shows that wherever ignorance exists there are spirit of disunion exists. Wherever light and education exist, there attachment to the Union existed.[2]

James P. Wickersham, a Republican Representative from Pennsylvania, added:

What can education do for the non-slaveholding whites of the South? Among this class are some intelligent men. But the great majority are deplorably ignorant. More ignorant than the slaves themselves. ... It was this ignorance that enabled the rebel leaders to create a prejudice in the minds of this class of persons against the North and to induce them to enlist in their armies. ... As long as they are ignorant they will remain tools of political demagogues and therefore be incapable of self-government. They must be educated; the duty is imperative. No state that has passed an act of secession should be allowed to take its former place in the Union without having first incorporated into its constitution a provision for the establishment of a free school system.[3]

Bureau of Education Absorbs Freedmen's Bureau.

By law the Freedmen's Bureau was to expire by 1872, but this did not happen. It lives on to this day in a disguised form. U.S. Representative Samuel Arnell of Tennessee said, relating to legislation which had just passed Congress, that the bill provided for the transfer of the education division of the Freedmen's Bureau to the Bureau of Education.

> The reasons for the passage of this bill were that the educational interests of the South require further aid ... that all funds now in the Treasury of the United States placed to the account of the Commissioner of the Bureau of Refugees, Freedmen, and Abandoned Lands, be transferred to the states for educational purposes, with special preference to aiding in the establishment of common schools among freedmen and refugees, and the clerks in the education division of the Freedmen's Bureau be transferred to and retained by the Bureau of Education.[4]

William Torrey Harris: Philosophy vs. The New Psychology.

The fourth Commissioner of the Bureau of Education was William Torrey Harris, from 1889 to 1906. Harris began as a teacher, then a principal, then the superintendent of St. Louis schools. Under his direction these schools were transformed from a backwater system to one of the best in America. This is why he became Commissioner.

Harris was also a serious philosopher, in an era when the United States was viewed, from Europe, as a crude frontier culture. While teaching in St. Louis, Harris published a magazine called *The Journal of Speculative Philosophy*. He was a disciple of Hegel. His followers were known as the St. Louis Hegelians. There was a strong religious and mystical tone to his viewpoint.

Paradoxically, the Bureau of Education's use of physio-psychology, comparative anatomy and child-centered education were the antithesis of all that Harris believed in. They linked animals to man instead of man being in God's image.

Yet under Harris's stewardship the Bureau of Education and its physiological research expanded enormously and reached into every tax-supported school in the United States. Ironically Harris simultaneously condemned and supported the "New Psychology. Here he denounces the empirical, experimental model developed at the agriculture stations, and the psychology that was the outcome of their laboratory work:

> One branch of the "New Psychology" is known as child study. The other is called 'physiological psychology.' ... The very concept of free will is impossible on the basis of empirical thinking [i.e., experience]. Coleridge defined empiricism as dealing with causal relations between objects, finding causal relations everywhere but no self-

activity or will .... Moral responsibility and religion, all transcend experience and are formed by introspection. ... It is their application which constitutes experience and experience would be impossible unless the mind had in itself these powers *a priori*, for these powers make experience possible. If we could not furnish the intuitions of infinite time and space, we could not perceive objects of experience, nor, unless we could furnish the category of causality we refer our sensations to objects as causes. Universal and necessary ideas are furnished by the mind itself and are not derived from experience. ... The "Old Psychology" is of priceless value, furnishing us with directive power, the regulative ideals of education, jurisprudence, politics, and the general conduct of life.[5]

Yet Harris contradicted himself and promoted the New Psychology based on physiological research:

In order to elevate from animals to civilization, man must know his environment, the racial influences, the different physical stages of man, his health, his mental health. All of which concerns education. That is why physiological psychology is important for child study, to bring out the soul at a tender age. Too much counting or repetitive work in school may make the soul mechanical. To keep the intellect out of the abyss of habit requires breaking through arrested development. ... The New Psychology will tell the teacher the point where growth stops and the mechanical begins. Brain and nerve study will promote this.[6]

---

1 *Annual Report of the Commissioner of the Bureau of Education for the Year 1868*, p. 2.

2 *Congressional Globe*, 41st Congress, Third Session, p. 1040.

3 Wickersham, p. 7

4 *Congressional Globe*, 41st Congress, Second Session, p. 2296

5 *Annual Report of the Commissioner of the Bureau of Education for the Year 1894*, p. 433.

6 *Annual Report of the Commissioner of the Bureau of Education for the Year 1897*, p. 437.

IX. Segregation by Fusing Church and State

WITH RECONSTRUCTION, the same process occurred in religion as in education and politics; the separation of blacks and whites. Congregations were split by force. This was to prevent the contamination of blacks by their former masters and neighbours. Historian Walter Fleming put it this way:

> With the advance of the Federal armies came the Northern churches. Territory gained by Northern armies was considered territory gained for the Northern churches. Northern ministers replaced Southerners, who were prohibited from preaching. The military authorities were especially hostile to the Methodist Episcopal Church South and Protestant Episcopal Church. The war was blamed on them .... In 1861 the Methodist Episcopal Church South had 200,000 black members. In 1866, 78,000 members. The policy, by Northern ministers, that all the Southern whites were enemies, destroyed and traditional black-white unity that had existed before the war.[1]

Freedmen chose their religion according to their politics. An Atlanta newspaper editor attributed the alienation of freedmen from Southern whites to the intrigues of Northern missionaries. The efforts of Southern Baptists had been thwarted, he said, by the influence from abroad, estranging the colored population from the whites for political ends. This originated with the industrious and widespread efforts of political and fanatical emissaries to alienate Baptists of African descent from their white brethren in the South – to induce their withdrawal from our churches – to lead them to forsake our ministry, and accept in lieu of it, the ministry of ignorant persons of their own color, of "loyal" and often irresponsible adventurers from a distance – to persuade them that they never heard the "full" or even the "true" gospel from the old instructors.[2]

Antebellum Churches Integrated.

Prior to the War for Southern Independence blacks had been members of the same churches as whites. Religious instruction had been given them by the families of their masters, by pastors of white churches, and by Negro ministers directed by churches, associations, and state conventions. ... Many white pastors had given considerable time to the religious interests of the slaves.[3]

One method of training black preachers which Southern Baptists employed was a plan known as Ministers Institutions. Baptists had used them since the early 19th century as a means of providing a modicum of instruction for preachers who lacked formal training. These institutes offered instruction in Bible and church polity.[4]

Antebellum Church Schisms Not Related to Slavery.

In the 1840s the Protestant sects in the United States began to split apart. It seemed the basic issue was slavery versus abolition. But fragmentation and schism was occurring all over the Protestant world. The first half of the 19th century witnessed tremendous religious conflicts. Old religious bodies divided and new ones arose. Presbyterians separated over doctrinal questions; Methodists divided over organization. The Oxford Movement in England gave impetus that put high churchmen in control of the Church of England and the Episcopal Church in the United States. Baptists separated into Campbellism, Hardshellism, and Freewillism. Abolition entered into the picture after 1830 but was merely one more fragmentation issue.

The history of the Baptist schism parallels the other sects, as well. In 1834 the Northern Baptist Board refused to take measures against Southern Baptists over slavery, but by the 1840s abolitionists first condemned slavery and then refused fellowship with those who had any connection to slavery.

In 1844 slaveholders were not permitted to be missionaries. A year later New York's *Baptist Reporter* advocated separation, but it was still not clear whether the cleavage would be geographical – North and South – or on the principle of isolating slaveholders only.

April 1845: The Virginia Baptist Foreign Mission Society was the first to separate: "From the Boston Board we separate not because we reside at the South but because they have adopted an unconstitutional and unscriptural principle to governing their future course."5

Post-War Churches Confiscated, then Segregated.

On November 20, 1863, the Secretary of War (Stanton) instructed Bishop Ames of the Northern Methodist Church to take over all the Southern churches. He would install ministers. These and other take-overs caused bitter controversies years after the war ended. In some cases, the Northern churches attempted to permanently hold Southern churches' property. "Loyal" prayers had to be given. Negroes were forcibly separated from Southern supervision. The policy of 'disintegration and absorption' was beginning.6

Another example was Reverend J.W. Horton, a representative of the American Home Mission Society New York, who visited New Orleans, "to look after Baptist interests." Finding the Coliseum Place Baptist Church neither desirous of his services, nor willing to surrender the house to him, he obtained a military order from General James Bowen, provost marshal, and thus forcibly obtained possession.7

One sect justified confiscation this way: Since Southern churches, as corporations, aided the rebellion, their property was liable to confiscation.8

Each Northern Sect Treats South Differently.

Southern Methodist churches were asked to make repentance by some ceremonious means for the crimes of which they had been judged guilty. "Until they ... repent before God and the nation in sackcloth and ashes for their offenses," said one Northern clergyman, "we believe them unfit for communion in Christ's church."[9]

Presbyterians said, Secession is a crime; withdrawal of Southern churches is a schism. The South was to be treated as a missionary field.[10]

Southern Baptist churches supported secession. When the Southern Baptist Convention met in Savannah in May 1861, it resolved:

> When any government is perverted from its proper design, becomes oppressive and abuses its power, the people have the right to change it. ... The Southern states have practically asserted the right of seceding from a Union so degenerated from that established by the Constitution, and they have framed for themselves a government based upon the principles of the original compact.[11]

With the end of hostilities, the American Baptist Home Mission, a Northern agency, made overtures to the Southern churches with talk of reunion. Such proposals incensed the former Confederates, largely because they felt the idea was government inspired and another phase of the occupation. Southerners had good reason for this feeling. For example, a resolution presented by the Reverend J.M. Pendleton, a Northern minister, defined suitable preachers for the South as men of unquestionable loyalty to the government of the United

States. Southern Baptists considered Pendleton a carpetbagger on a spiritual plane.[12]

Episcopalians were the only denomination that was conciliatory. Since no test oaths or any other conditions were required for Southern churches to re-unite with the North, the Federal government and the military were more hostile to this sect. This increased when the Episcopal Bishop Richard H. Wilmer would not give the appropriate Reconstruction prayer to the North and President Johnson. He and his clergymen were suspended from conducting services until they would show allegiance to the government. Then the churches were closed by troops when Wilmer said the civil authorities could not interfere in religious matters. When the congregation attempted to meet in a school building, they were dispersed by troops with bayonets. Negroes who joined this denomination were ostracized and left alone in sickness and death.

Northern Churches Merge with Carpetbagger States.

When Congress prolonged the life of the Freedmen's Bureau in 1866, it directed Commissioner O.O. Howard at all times to cooperate with private benevolent associations ... in aid of the freedmen and appropriated $500,000 for schools ... including construction, rental and repairs.[13]

With this legislation, the material donation of the government to church schools increased. This was a direct subsidy to religious endeavors. As a result, federal policy became church dogma, and church officials became federal employees. Northern religious leaders passed beyond the common ranks in the Freedmen's Bureau administrative structure to reach stations of power and dignity. Clayton Fisk of the Methodist Church North directed Bureau affairs in the combined jurisdiction of Tennessee and Kentucky. At different times clergymen held state superintendent of education positions under the Freedmen's Bureau in Virginia, Florida, Tennessee, and Alabama, according to Ralph Ernest Morrow in his work *Northern Methodists and Reconstruction*.[14]

Morrow added that many Northern clergymen were incurable Radicals who incorporated social dogmas and political tests into their church creeds,[15] while Henry C. Dean stated that "Every innovation by the army, the Executive or Congress was adopted as a new canon of religion, or a new article of religious faith."[16]

The ability of Northern clergymen to furnish grist for Republican mills was emphasized during the Congressional investigation of the Klan in 1871, according to Morrow:

> In a half-dozen Southern states, Negroes or white preachers of the Northern churches testified with varying effectiveness before the exceedingly partisan joint committee, but the most sensational of them was Alabama presiding Methodist elder, Arad S. Lakin, who had emigrated from Ohio in late 1865, had executed earlier missions for the Radicals. Aside from the formation of Loyal League [Union League] cells among the Negroes, he compiled a documentary pamphlet on outrages in the South of which the Republicans distributed over a million copies

during the 1868 campaign. Lakin's committee testimony, many hours long and replete with illustrations of Southern barbarities, was the focal point of the inquiry into Alabama affairs, and won for the parson considerable notice in both majority and minority reports of the investigations. To the Republicans his words and documents were incontestable evidence that religious loyalty could not live safely in the Southern states. The Democratic evaluation, although no more judicious, was considerably different. The Democratic minority scorched Lakin as a "slanderer ... brimful of gall, bitterness and falsehood" who "'seemed to be incapable of speaking the plain unvarnished truth.'" [17]

---

1 Fleming, p. 647.

2 *Christian Index* (Atlanta), June 10, 1869, p. 90.

3 William Wright Barnes, *The Southern Baptist Convention 1843-1953* (Nashville: Broadman Press, 1954), p. 60.

4 *Southern Baptist Convention Proceedings*, 1875, Barnes, p. 73.

5 Barnes, p. 26.

6 Fleming, p. 228.

7 Barnes, p. 52.

8 Ralph Ernest Morrow, *Northern Methodists and Reconstruction* (East Lansing, Michigan: Michigan State University Press, 1956), p. 40.

9 Morrow, p. 69.

10 Fleming, p. 640.

11 *Journal of the Congress of the Confederate States of America*, May 17, 1861, p. 237.

12 O.K. and Marjorie Armstrong, *The Indomitable Baptists* (Garden City: Doubleday & Co., 1967), p. 212.

13 Morrow, p. 163.

14 Morrow, p. 154.

15 Fleming, p. 637.

16 Henry Clay Dean, *Crimes of the Civil War and the Curse of the Funding System* (Baltimore: J. Wesley & Bro., 1869), p. 178.

17 Morrow, pp. 241-242.

X. Conclusion: Reconstruction Continues Into the 21st Century

Hunting Klansmen: Then Relates to Now.

WITCH HUNTS in the Reconstruction South to ferret out racists and Klansmen have steadily expanded over the past century so that Uncle Sam now searches for racists, Klansmen, Copperheads, and a dozen new categories of so-called subversives who are politically, socially, and/or sexually incorrect in every state of the Union. These contemporary persecutions are still based on the post-war Reconstruction laws that have never been expunged from the statute books. Quite the contrary, they are vastly more destructive now. A multitude of federal and state agencies have been created to insure that each citizen's thoughts and deeds are always perfect.

Jabez Curry of Alabama made the following comments about the brutality inflicted on the South in the 1860s, but it is just as true in the new millennium:

> These men, with star chamber powers, and views incurably hostile to the character of the [Southern] people, began and prosecuted their work exposing, uncovering nakedness, exposing peculiarities and weakness, transforming objectionable exceptions and incidents into rules of life and characteristics of a people, searching

with microscope eye every fault, heralding every intemperate expression, perverting every utterance. ... The Czar of Russia or Sultan of Turkey would not have the temerity, the cruelty, to place their subjects under such a strain and burden.[1]

John Dewey's Grandchildren.

In the 1880s John Dewey took the physio-psychology and comparative anatomy experiments of the Morrill Act and turned them into an educational philosophy called Progressivism. Supposedly it would help teach for a new radical Utopian egalitarian social order. Progressivism would teach democracy to those who hated it – those racist, rebellious Southerners. In the 20th century his ideas dominated all tax-supported schools throughout the entire United States.

Dewey's conception of democracy was really more like dictatorship. Democracy requires stable law. Dewey held the opposite position: "The venture to which democracy has committed itself in response to the needs of the moment, is in accordance with the ascertained truths of the moment."[2]

He believed that democracy meant change, but change for the sake of change creates social chaos by destroying the constancy of law. This leads to dictatorship. Naively Dewey said: "The education for democracy is ... constant change ... continuous reconstruction for social ends."[3] Democracy was defined by the political needs of the moment.

Progressive History.

History is an explosive, dangerous subject. It can tell a story of unchanging truths which are at odds with the politically correct. Progressivism erased the historical past through its New History, which paralleled the New Psychology. Both erased the cultural past. Dewey believed that the questions of the past and precedence of origins is quite subordinate to guidance and control amid future possibilities. The present is the true past, he added. History should be an imaginative creation designed by the "educator."[4]

The trendy curriculum ideas of contemporary schools are merely the reworkings of what was *avant-garde* in Progressive schools at the turn of the 20th century.

Speciesism.

Darwin and comparative anatomy still have not lost their premier position in the modern classroom. Children are taught that man is just another beast in the animal chain. This reduces children's motivation in the same relation to man's reduced significance.

Whole Wordism.

Following the anti-book ideals of Progressivism (which promoted hands-on manual skill), today students are taught entire words and sentences first instead of the alphabet, so they can only relate to what is directly in front of them here and now. They can only perform a specific task, but without mastering the basic letters they do not have a wider understanding.

New Textbooks.

They teach what supposedly interests kids, not what is crucial to learn. This parallels the physiology-based, child-centered experiments of the 19th century. Writing skills are judged for meaning, not grammar or spelling. This promotes illiteracy.

Whole Math.

This is the numerical equivalent of whole wordism. Concepts first, basics follow. Social policy agendas lurk behind this. Currently there is a substantial difference in scores between the races and sexes when traditional math is taught. Whole math erases the difference, giving the illusion of equality for all.

Confiscation for Off-Budget Funding.

Law works by precedent. Current legislative enactments are based on law created in the distant past.

Present day misdemeanor arrests often lead to the total confiscation of a person's private property, well above the legal limits of the crime. Massive property takeovers by the IRS are justified for small income tax irregularities. These actions base their legality on Reconstruction-era statutes.

Today, as then, the money generated by the sale of confiscated property is channeled into clandestine funds. This practice is so widespread it has a name: Off-Budget Government. It is so immense that some analysts believe that these hidden budgets match that which is revealed in the Federal budget: $1.5 trillion annually. State and local governments follow the same pattern. And to think, it all started with the Freedmen's Bureau. Reconstruction is still very much with us.

Segregation by Force Begets Integration by Force.

Uncle Sam has come full circle. He created segregation by fraud, force, and violence, then blamed Southerners for those deeds. Now he employs busing, gerrymandering of election districts, the police, the national guard, the courts, confiscation, and the threat of incarceration to achieve a coercive, integrated, egalitarian society through an arbitrary ratio of blacks to whites. This is totally in keeping with the utopian dream of the Radical Republican carpetbaggers and congressmen.

Churches Spread National Policy, Not God.

Church and state are still linked together, just like in the 1860s. The laws of Congress, not biblical laws, are still proclaimed from the pulpit, even when they are in direct conflict with basic Christian doctrine.

Preachers promote and congregations accept legalized homosexual marriages, as one example, even when it is clear that congressional anti-discrimination edicts view the Bible as a hate book for condemning it. Inescapably this will draw Christian denominations under ever-tightening regulations, ever more diligent scrutiny, until every church becomes a branch of the federal government that informs the public of today's immortal truths from the lips of the president.

---

1 Jabez L.M. Curry Papers, fragment of a letter from Curry to an unknown person, The Library of Congress.

2 John Blewett, editor, *John Dewey: His Thought and Influence* (New York: Fordham University Press, 1960), p. 89.

3 *Ibid.*, p. 105.

4 *Ibid.*, pp. 152, 153, 147.

About the Author

JOHN CHODES is a playwright, biographer, and historian. His books include, among others, *The Myth of America's Military Power (1972)*; *Corbitt: The Story of Ted Corbitt, Long Distance Runner* (1973), which won the "Journalistic Excellence Award" from the Road Runners Club of America; *Bruce Jenner* (1976), which has sold over 200,000 copies; *Destroying the Republic: Jabez Curry and the Re-education of the Old South* (2005); *Horatio Seymour: New York's Governor Attacks Abe Lincoln's War* (2011); *In Praise of the Free Market and Peace* (2012); *Abe Lincoln's Secret War Against the North* (2012); and *Washington's KKK: The Union League During Southern Reconstruction* (2016).

Mr. Chodes has published more than 100 articles in various books and journals (including *Chronicles, The Freeman, Social Justice Review, The New York Tribune* and others). He was technical advisor for the movie "Marathon Man." He was Communications Director for the New York Libertarian Party for which he received an award for Meritorious Service. His greatest distinction perhaps is as a dramatist. Eight of his plays, mostly on historical subjects, have been produced off-Broadway.

A lifelong resident of New York, Mr. Chodes became interested in the history of the War Between the States and the South when he looked into the U.S. Army invasion and occupation of his city during that war. He writes that he is interested in free trade, limited government, the privatisation of education, and a deregulated economy — principles of the Old South.

Available from Shotwell

Southern Studies

A Legion of Devils: Sherman in South Carolina by Karen Stokes

Annals of the Stupid Party: Republicans Before Trump by Clyde N. Wilson (The Wilson Files 2)

Dismantling the Republic by Jerry C. Brewer

Dixie Rising: Rules for Rebels by James R. Kennedy

Emancipation Hell: The Tragedy Wrought By Lincoln's Emancipation Proclamation by Kirkpatrick Sale

Lies My Teacher Told Me: The True History of the War for Southern Independence by Clyde N. Wilson

Maryland, My Maryland: The Cultural Cleansing of a Small Southern State by Joyce Bennett.

Nullification: Reclaiming Consent of the Governed by Clyde N. Wilson (The Wilson Files 2)

Punished with Poverty: The Suffering South by James R. & Walter D. Kennedy

Southern Independence. Why War? - The War to Prevent Southern Independence by Dr. Charles T. Pace

Southerner, Take Your Stand! by John Vinson

Washington's KKK: The Union League During Southern Reconstruction by John Chodes.

When the Yankees Come: Former South Carolina Slaves Remember Sherman's Invasion. Edited with Introduction by Paul C. Graham

The Yankee Problem: An American Dilemma by Clyde N. Wilson (The Wilson Files 1)

Fiction

GREEN ALTAR BOOKS
(Literary Imprint)

A New England Romance & Other SOUTHERN Stories by Randall Ivey

Tiller (Clay Bank County, IV) by James Everett Kibler

GOLD-BUG MYSTERIES
(Mystery & Thriller Imprint)

To Jekyll and Hide by Martin L. Wilson

Publisher's Note

IF YOU ENJOYED THIS BOOK or found it useful, interesting, or informative, we'd be very grateful if you would post a brief review of it on the retailer's website.

In the current political and cultural climate, it is important that we get accurate, Southern friendly material into the hands of our friends and neighbors. *Your support can really make a difference* in helping us unapologetically celebrate and defend our Southern heritage, culture, history, and home!

For more information, or to sign-up for notification of forthcoming titles (and receive a FREE eBook), please visit us at

SHOTWELLPUBLISHING.COM

Southern without Apology.

www.ingramcontent.com/pod-product-compliance
Lightning Source LLC
Chambersburg PA
CBHW070653050426
42451CB00008B/338